VEHICLES

AIRPLANES

Written by Bethany Latham

Genius Kid

sales@northstareditions.com | 888-417-0195

Library of Congress Control Number:
2025943087

ISBN
979-8-89471-065-5 (library bound)
979-8-89471-085-3 (paperback)
979-8-89471-121-8 (epub)
979-8-89471-105-8 (hosted ebook)

Printed in the United States of America
Mankato, MN
012026

Written by:
Bethany Latham

Edited by:
Rebecca Phillips-Bartlett

Designed by:
Rob Delph

Photo Credits – Images courtesy of Shutterstock.com, unless otherwise stated.

Cover – Karrrtinki, next143, EB Adventure Photography, Sergey Ogaryov, aappp, Dushlik, Kamira, Ensuper, Kateryna Mashkevych, Mr Doomits, Engineer studio, Dja65, Shutterstock-Pixelsquid, CHAINFOTO24, cunaplusr. 2–3 – Rob Wilson, Caftor, John Selway. 4–5 – Caftor, vaalaa, Dushlik, Travis Potter, Rob Wilson, VanderWolf Images. 6–7 – Roman Samborskyi, Bychykhin Olexandr, StudioSmart, naratrip2. 8–9 – Everett Collection, photoshooter2015, chrisdorney, J J Osuna Caballero, Natatal, John Selway, Ground Picture. 10–11 – eka.viation, EB Adventure Photography, Dushlik, Sergey Ogaryov, aappp. 12–13 – vaalaa, Kostafly. 14–15 – Svitlana Hulko, SF photo, Media_works, Lithium366, Jetstream Rider. 16–17 – Rashevskyi Viacheslav, shaineast. 18–19 – Ozgur Coskun, litabit, T.B. photo, Mario Hagen, Mark_D. 20–21 – Ronen Fefer, SUNDAYUA, Olga Popova, Dushlik. 22–23 – Kamira, Zyryanova Irina, Dr_Flash, BearFotos, Engineer studio, Dushlik. 24 – VanderWolf Images.

CONTENTS

Words that look like this can be found in the glossary on page 24.

AIRPLANES

Airplanes are amazing machines. They can help us travel quickly over states and oceans. Have you ever flown in an airplane?

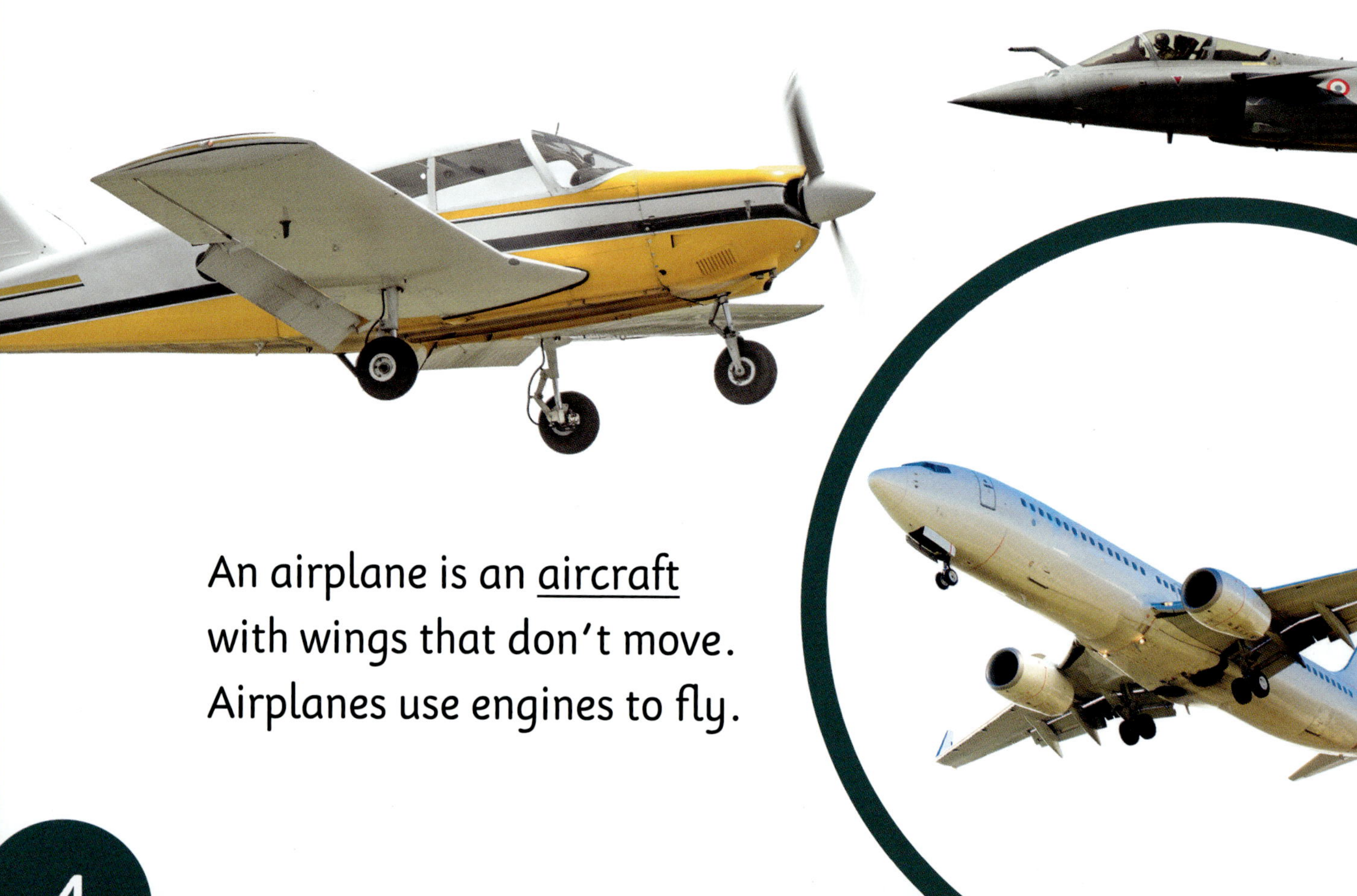

An airplane is an aircraft with wings that don't move. Airplanes use engines to fly.

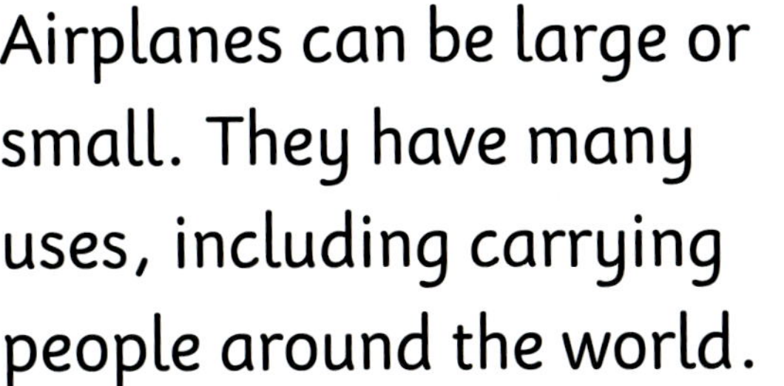

Airplanes can be large or small. They have many uses, including carrying people around the world.

Airplanes are faster than many other types of transportation.

Can you imagine a world without airplanes?

KEY WORDS

Here are some key words about airplanes that every genius kid should learn.

PILOT

A pilot is a person who flies an airplane.

RUNWAY

The runway is a long, straight strip of flat ground where airplanes take off and land.

COCKPIT

The cockpit is where the pilot sits to fly the airplane. It is at the front of the airplane.

AERODYNAMICS

Aerodynamics is the science of flight. It explains how objects move through the air and how airplanes fly.

DID YOU KNOW?

Aero means "relating to aircraft." *Dynamics* means "relating to movement."

A TIMELINE OF AIRPLANES

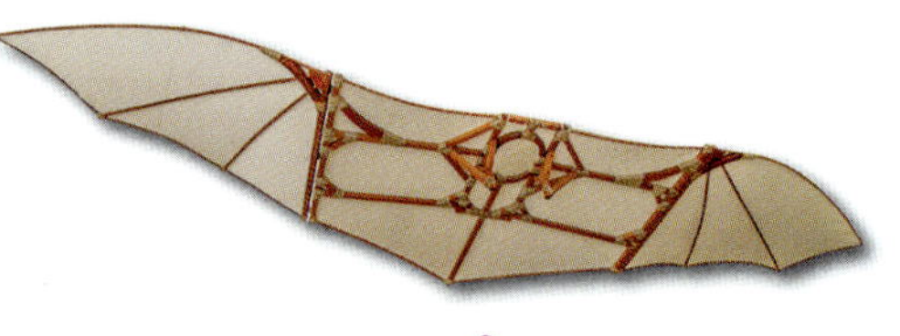

1480s
Leonardo da Vinci designed a flying machine called an ornithopter.

1843
George Cayley designed a biplane glider. It had two unmoving sets of wings.

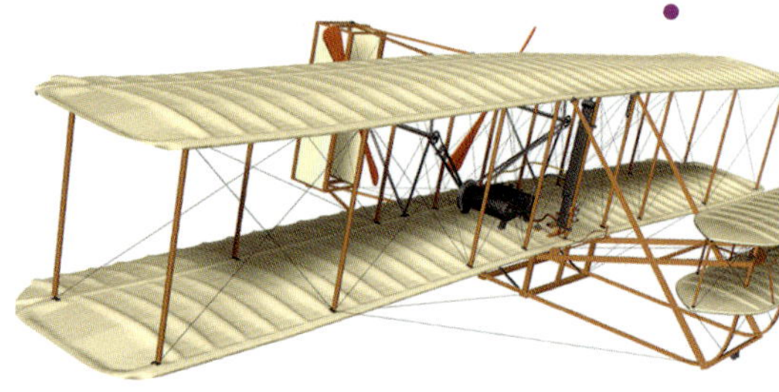

1903
Orville and Wilbur Wright were the first people to fly a heavier-than-air airplane. They flew for less than one minute.

1932

Amelia Earhart became the first woman to fly alone across the Atlantic Ocean.

1937

Frank Whittle built the jet engine.

1976

The Concorde was a <u>supersonic</u> airplane. It began flying passengers.

Now

Many people fly in airplanes.

TYPES OF AIRPLANES

There are many different kinds of airplanes.

Jumbo jets are the largest passenger airplanes in the world. Some can carry up to 850 people.

Jumbo jet

Biplanes were the first kind of airplane. They have two sets of wings with one on top of the other.

Biplane

Cargo planes carry items instead of people.

Cargo plane

Seaplane

Seaplanes are airplanes that can take off and land on water.

Fighter jets are used by the military.

Fighter jet

AIRPLANE PARTS

The fuselage is the body of the airplane. It is where passengers sit.

On the outside, most airplanes have the same parts.

The front of the plane is called the nose.

The landing gear helps the plane take off and land smoothly. Most landing gear includes wheels.

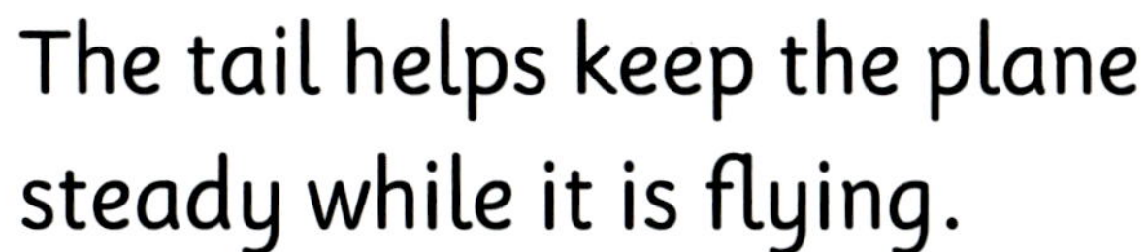

The tail helps keep the plane steady while it is flying.

The wings help the airplane fly by creating lift.

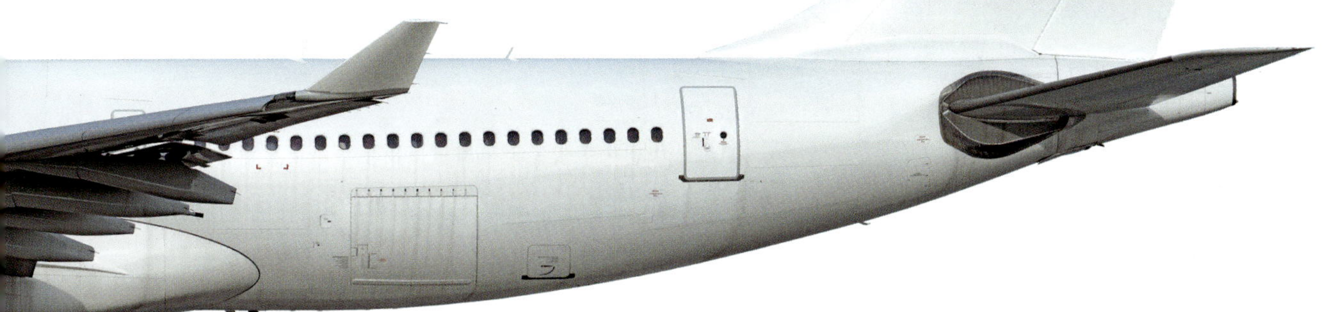

Some planes have propellers. They are attached to the engine. They spin to create thrust.

IN THE COCKPIT

On the inside, airplanes have many parts to help them fly.

The stick or yoke is the airplane's steering wheel. The pilot uses it to move the plane up, down, left, and right.

Yoke

The pedals control the rudder on the tail. The rudder helps steer the plane.

Pedals

DID YOU KNOW?
The cockpit is also called the flight deck.

The throttle controls the power and speed of the airplane.

Throttle

Flight instruments

The instrument panel gives the pilot information about the airplane while it is flying, such as its speed.

Pilots use radios to communicate with others while flying.

Radio

INSIDE THE ENGINE

Many airplanes use jet engines. Jet engines work by creating thrust.

Blades suck air into the front of the engine. The air is squeezed and pushed. Then the air is sprayed with fuel and lit on fire.

The burning fuel and air create gas. The gas bursts out the back of the engine very quickly.

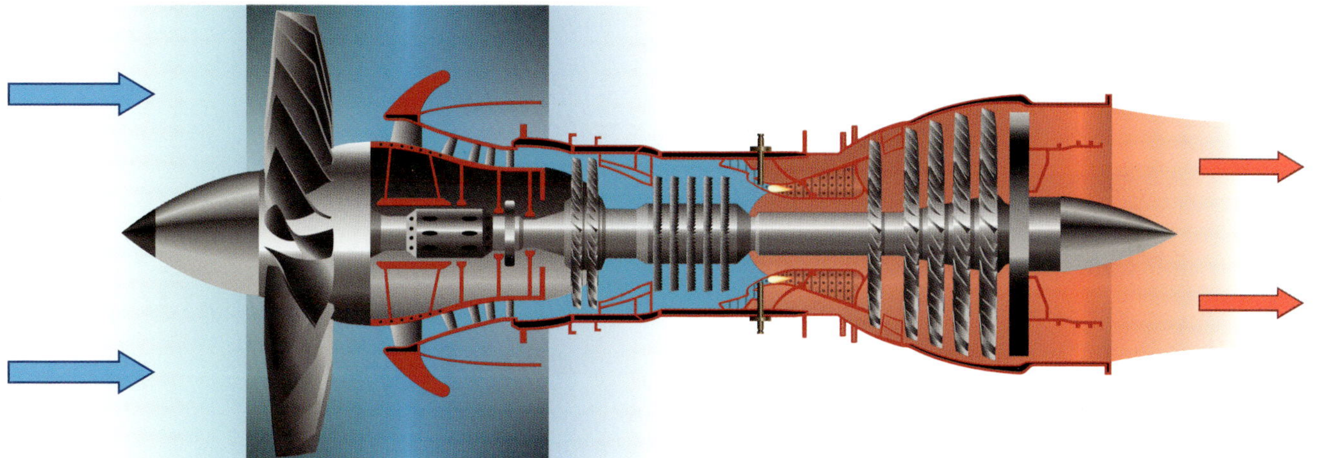

This gas shoots backward while the engine thrusts the airplane forward through the air.

DID YOU KNOW?

You can remember how a jet engine works using four words: suck, squeeze, bang, blow.

SAFETY FIRST

There are many things in an airplane that keep passengers safe. Most are only used in emergencies.

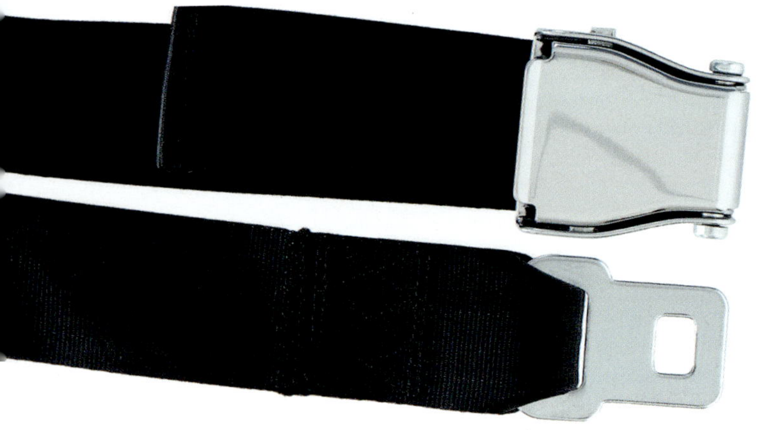

Seatbelts stop passengers' bodies from moving too much during turbulence.

Oxygen masks help passengers breathe safely if the air pressure drops.

Life vests help passengers float if the plane lands in water.

Emergency slides help passengers exit the plane safely if they need to leave quickly.

Wheel chocks stop the airplane from rolling when it is on the ground. They fit under the wheels.

BELIEVE IT OR NOT!

A Boeing 747 jet airplane is made up of around six million different parts.

The Concorde could fly from New York to London in under three hours. Planes today take about seven hours.

The first person to fly alone across the Atlantic Ocean was Charles A. Lindbergh. He made the flight in 1927 in an airplane called the *Spirit of St. Louis*.

Traveling by airplane is the safest method of transport.

ARE YOU A GENIUS KID?

Now you have lots of interesting airplane facts to impress your friends and family with. But first, it is time to test your knowledge. Are you really a genius kid?

Check back through the book if you are not sure.

1. What is the name of the first woman who flew alone across the Atlantic Ocean?
2. What is the name of an airplane's steering wheel?
3. How many parts are in a Boeing 747 jet airplane?

Answers:
1. Amelia Earhart
2. stick or yoke
3. around six million

GLOSSARY

aircraft a machine that can fly

air pressure how much force air has when it is compressed into a space

communicate to pass information between two or more things

fuel something that can be used to make energy or power something

gas a thing that is like air, which spreads out to fill any space available

lift an upward force

military the armed forces of a country, such as the army, air force, and navy

supersonic able to move faster than the speed of sound

thrust a force that makes an object move forward

turbulence the irregular and swift motion of air currents

INDEX